W9-DDV-475

30108000186556

BLACK TUESDAY

The Stock Market Crash of 1929

BY BARBARA SILBERDICK FEINBERG

Spotlight on American History
The Millbrook Press • Brookfield, Connecticut

Dedicated to the memory of Charlotte Shemansky,
who took such loving care of
my brother and me when we were children.

In writing this book, I consulted with the following people and would like to
thank them for helping me to locate research materials or to better understand
how to convey to young readers the terms and concepts used in this book:
Gina Cane, Monroe Firestone, Suzanne Freedman,
Carol Kochman, Naomi Neft, and Menasha Tausner.

Cover photograph courtesy of Brown Brothers

Photographs courtesy of Bettmann Archive: pp. 6, 24, 30, 33 (photo
courtesy of the FDR Library), 37; © Sandra Baker, Liaison International:
p. 11; UPI/Bettmann: pp. 13, 16, 20 (both), 36 (both), 41, 50; Herbert
Hoover Presidential Library: pp. 39, 48 (both); National Museum of
American Art/Washington, DC/Art Resource, NY: pp. 52–53.

Library of Congress Cataloging-in-Publication Data
Feinberg, Barbara Silberdick.
Black Tuesday : the stock market crash of 1929 /
Barbara Silberdick Feinberg.
p.   cm.—(Spotlight on American history)
Includes bibliographical references and index.
Summary: Discusses events contributing to the 1929 stock market crash,
the Great Depression that followed, and steps taken to revive the nation.
ISBN 1-56294-574-2
1. New York Stock Exchange—History—Juvenile literature.
2. Depressions 1929—United States—Juvenile literature.
[1. United States—Economic conditions 1918–1945.   2. New York Stock
Exchange—History.   3. Depressions 1929.] I. Title. II. Series.
HB3717 1929.F44 1995 338.5′4′097309043—dc20 94-44439 CIP AC

Contents

Black Tuesday

Variety *ran the headline, "Wall St. Lays an Egg," on October 30, 1929.*
The article reports with a dramatic flourish, "Tragedy, despair and
ruination spell the story of countless thousands of marginal stock traders."

CHAPTER ONE

"WALL STREET LAYS AN EGG"

At ten o'clock in the morning on Tuesday, October 29, 1929, New York Stock Exchange Superintendent William Crawford banged his gavel to open the market as he did every day. Immediately, huge blocks of stocks were put up for sale at the Exchange's seventeen trading posts. The floor was soon littered with crumpled pieces of paper, trampled by people racing from trading post to trading post to place orders to sell stock. At 10:03 A.M., 650,000 shares of U.S. Steel had been dumped on the market, and the stock's price per share plummeted from $205 to $179. During the first six minutes of trading, General Electric stock dropped a dollar every ten seconds. Westinghouse lost two dollars a minute during the first quarter of an hour. At trading post six, two clerks started fighting during the rush to sell American Can stock.

Just thirty minutes after the New York Stock Exchange opened, 3,259,800 shares had been sold for a loss of over $2 billion. By eleven o'clock, the stocks were being sold for whatever price they could bring. A bright messenger boy for the Exchange put in a bid for White Sewing Machine Company at a dollar a share; it had already fallen from a high of $48 per share to $11.25 on Monday. He got it!

The NYSE's communication systems were quickly swamped with orders to sell before the prices of shares fell even farther. Private lines linked the Exchange to brokerage houses in New York's financial district and to other markets around the nation. The wave of selling spread quickly. Shareholders all over the United States had flocked to their brokers and watched in disbelief as the tumbling stock prices were posted on chalkboards. The value of their shares continued to drop, so they decided to cut their losses.

As a result, brokers across the country flooded the NYSE's 1,145 telephone operators with orders to sell shareholders' stock. The telephone operators passed the orders to a staff of 500 pages. Dressed in uniforms resembling those of military cadets, the pages rushed about with far from military precision to pass the orders to the trading posts.

With the ever-increasing number of sales, the overhead screens at the NYSE, which were supposed to project the latest prices quoted for the shares, began to fall behind. Tickertape machines printed out the latest stock quotations, or prices, in brokers' offices all over the nation, but they could not keep up with the rapid changes either. They soon quoted only the last digit of the price of each stock, which made it more difficult for brokers to keep track of the falling prices. Did a 3 mean 53, 43, 33, 23, 13, or just 3?

For every million shares traded, five hundred miles of tickertape ran through the machines. By noon, the number of shares that had changed hands exceeded eight million. An hour and a half later the number had risen to more than 12 million. Wastebaskets all over the United States were overflowing with the white ribbons of paper. In better times, tickertape had been thrown out of windows to cheer the nation's heroes as they paraded by, but now there was little to celebrate.

At noon, acting NYSE president Richard Whitney called a secret meeting of the Governors Committee to decide whether or not to shut down operations for the rest of the day. He did not wish to further alarm already frightened and confused shareholders. Instead of assembling in the Governing Committee Room, where they usually met, the governors slipped quietly away from the trading floor in groups of twos and threes to a small basement office where they nervously lit cigarettes and stubbed them out after a puff or two. Whitney later explained, "Panic was raging overhead on the [trading] floor. Every few minutes the latest prices were announced, with quotations moving swiftly and irreversibly downward." The governors decided to keep the Exchange open in the hope that the situation would improve.

The visitor's gallery was empty. It had been closed since Black Thursday, October 24, when a wave of frenzied selling had sent stock prices tumbling—a sign of things to come. On that day, a few wealthy bankers met at the offices of J. P. Morgan, a prestigious private banking house that had funded many huge industrial companies. The bankers formed a stock-purchasing group to prop up the falling market. At about 2:00 P.M., their agent, Richard Whitney, bid up the price of steel. This gave the market the boost

HOW THE STOCK MARKET WORKS

THE New York Stock Exchange (NYSE), founded in 1792, is the most important stock market in the United States. The 1,375 members of the NYSE represent their own brokerage firms and nonmember brokers across the country.

For a fee, brokers arrange trades in stocks and bonds. Stocks are shares in the ownership of businesses. Bonds are notes in which businesses or the government promise bondholders to repay money lent to them with interest (the cost of borrowing the money).

The process of buying and selling a stock resembles an auction, with the shares going to the highest bidder. On the floor of the NYSE, a broker with a customer's order to buy a certain number of shares calls out a bid, the current price or less, at a trading post specializing in that type of stock. Another member, with an order to sell a customer's shares, will either accept that offer or hold out for a higher price. The two members may bargain until they reach a mutually satisfactory price. It is then recorded as the current price of the stock, which the buyer must pay and the seller must receive.

The price of stocks is determined by the number of shares available for sale and the number of people eager to buy them. If many people want to buy a stock, its price usually rises. If many people want to sell it, the stock's price usually drops. That is why sellers may get more or less than they paid for their shares in the first place. The supply of stocks for sale and the demand for them depends on a number of different things: how well businesses are performing and what their future prospects are; how well the economy is doing; what events are taking place nationally and internationally; and how the public feels about the future.

The trading floor of the New York Stock Exchange today.

it needed, and stocks gradually resumed their climb. On October 29, there was little that Whitney could do. The sell-off was too rapid and too severe.

By early afternoon, about ten thousand people had made their way to Wall Street. This eight-block strip at the foot of Manhattan Island served as the financial center of the United States and the home of the NYSE. These worried shareholders and curious New Yorkers had heard troubling rumors that the stock market was going to crash. Many were afraid their stocks would become worthless. As far as two blocks away from the Stock Exchange, they could hear the shouts of traders yelling out orders to sell. They feared the rumors were true. To help the city's patrolmen control the jittery crowd, twenty mounted police were rushed to the financial district. Nearby Trinity Church was soon overflowing with frightened New Yorkers seeking comfort.

Another rumor soon began to spread—that vast numbers of shareholders were committing suicide because they had lost all they owned in the stock market. A woman did jump to her death from the roof of New York's Equitable Building, and the frequent wail of ambulance sirens could be heard through the streets of the city. Most ambulances, however, were sent to false alarms. In one instance, a would-be suicide turned out to be a window washer sitting on a ledge, taking a break from his job. Actually, the suicide rate did not rise significantly either during or after the Crash. It had been higher during the summer when the market was doing well. Nevertheless, the public was ready to believe that stock market losses drove many people to kill themselves.

By the time the NYSE closed at 5:32 P.M., a record 16,410,030 shares had been traded in one day. The average prices of fifty leading stocks had dropped 40 points a share. This meant

The day after the stock market crash, a car is put up for sale. This sort of desperate act would be a common sight in the days and months to come.

that an investor who had bought a stock for $100 a share could only get $60 a share for it. All told, the market lost about $14 billion in one day. One Wall Street broker remembered staying late at the office: "It must have been ten, eleven o'clock before we got the final reports. It was like a thunder clap. Everybody was stunned. Nobody knew what it was all about."

The next day, October 30, the show business newspaper *Variety* ran a banner headline, "Wall St. Lays An Egg." The wave of selling that took place on October 29, Black Tuesday, marked the end of good times. (Stocks, however, did not reach their lowest prices until November 13.) Why did the crash happen? How would it affect the American people? Would their lives be very different? They would soon find out.

CHAPTER TWO

"A CAR IN EVERY BACKYARD"

The year 1929 had started out on a promising note. A new president, Republican Herbert C. Hoover, was sworn in, insisting, "I have no fears for the future of our country."

Why shouldn't good times continue? So far, the roaring twenties had been rowdy, carefree, and noisy. Never were Americans more determined to have fun. The era was known for madcap stunts such as contests to see who could sit on top of a flagpole the longest or who could swallow the most goldfish. More important records were set, too. In 1929, a construction contract was signed to build what would then be the world's tallest skyscraper, the Empire State Building in New York City. Lieutenant Commander Richard E. Byrd made the first flight over the South Pole. Only two years earlier, Charles E. Lindbergh had made the first trans-Atlantic solo flight, arriving in Paris thirty-three hours after he left New York.

A Swedish pole vault champion and his partner dance in a Charleston contest in Los Angeles, 1926. During the twenties, records, stunts, and competitions were the rage.

In the past, Americans had admired men who were in charge of large organizations, made important discoveries, or risked their lives to accomplish great things. Although people still looked up to automaker Henry Ford, inventor Thomas Edison, and pilot Charles Lindbergh, a new type of hero—the celebrity—was on the rise. Movie stars, like leading man Rudolph Valentino, became popular idols. (Sadly, Valentino died in 1926 at the age of thirty-one, but his fame continued to spread.) Outstanding athletes, like Babe Ruth, with his record-breaking sixty homers in 1927, were worshiped by their fans.

Women were developing a new sense of importance and independence. Since 1920, they had voted in elections, gone to work in greater numbers, and had even smoked cigarettes in public. Their clothing reflected their newfound freedoms. They rejected the restrictive styles of the past. No longer would they be laced into tight corsets to give them tiny waistlines, or wear long skirts that limited their movements. They became "flappers," dressed in shapeless dresses that barely skimmed their knees. They also "bobbed" their hair to chin length, letting it toss freely instead of piling it up on top of their heads, secured by numerous hairpins. In 1929, they were delighted when Helen Wills won her third Wimbledon tennis championship.

Music captured the rhythm of a people on the move, eager to have fun. Throughout the decade, George Gershwin wrote hit musical comedies like *Funny Face* and serious compositions, such as *Rhapsody in Blue*. Jazz greats Duke Ellington and Louis Armstrong were among popular performers of the 1920s. In 1929, Americans first began to hum "Singin' in the Rain," a popular song still heard today. Not only did men and women listen to the music, they kicked up their heels and danced the Charleston and the Black Bottom.

Americans loved to go to the movies. Audiences laughed at Charlie Chaplin's little tramp, Harold Lloyd's daredevil feats, and Buster Keaton's deadpan expressions on the silent screen. They sighed when they saw "America's Sweetheart," Mary Pickford, the innocent girl next door, and Gloria Swanson, a slinky sex symbol. In 1927, *The Jazz Singer* opened, letting moviegoers actually hear popular entertainer Al Jolson's voice. The next year, Mickey Mouse made his first appearance on the screen. The first Academy Awards were presented in 1929. *Wings*, the story of two American pilots during World War I, was chosen as best picture. Made in 1927–1928, it was the first and last silent film to be honored. By 1929, filmmakers were busy converting their studios to produce talking pictures. For those who liked to make home movies, Kodak began to manufacture 16-millimeter color film in 1929.

Radio programs also delighted the American public. Since 1920, when the nation's first commercial station, KDKA, went on the air in Pittsburgh, the listening audience had more than tripled. In 1922, there were only 60,000 households with radios, but by 1929 that number had swelled to 10,250,000. The speeches of presidents Calvin Coolidge and Herbert Hoover had already been broadcast to the public by 1929, and the popular radio comedy show *Amos 'n Andy* began its long run. Originally two white men played the African-American characters, but in later years, their roles were taken over by blacks. In 1928, station WGY in Schenectady had started the first regularly scheduled television broadcasts, but it would take another twenty years before the idea really caught on.

*T*HERE WAS, HOWEVER, a darker side to the decade. Since 1920, it had been illegal for Americans to buy or sell alcoholic beverages. To meet the demand for these forbidden drinks, bootleggers smuggled in bottles of alcohol from Canada and Europe or brewed their own concoctions to sell to eager customers. People also flocked to speakeasies, illegal, private clubs where they could buy a drink. Often gangsters took control of illegal liquor supplies. There were wars between rival gangs for control of this profitable business. On February 14, 1929, members of George "Bugsy" Moran's gang in Chicago were ambushed by their rivals and shot with submachine guns. Crime boss Al "Scarface" Capone supposedly ordered this "St. Valentine's Day Massacre." Since there was no proof of his involvement, law enforcement officials were only able to charge him with a minor crime. In May 1929, Capone was sentenced to a year in prison for carrying a concealed weapon.

Racism also marred the decade. Americans grew increasingly suspicious of people whose lifestyles or appearances were different from their own. By 1929, immigration laws had discouraged eastern and southern Europeans from coming to the United States. Earlier, many of these immigrants had flocked to American cities, where they clung to their Old World ways of living. Now they were no longer welcome because they seemed to be an economic threat, and they did not fit into white middle-class America. Asians were also excluded.

In the mid-1920s, the Ku Klux Klan, a racist, white supremacist group, preyed on blacks, Jews, and immigrants. Mobs of white men still lynched blacks on trumped-up charges. In 1920, fifty-three African Americans were killed by lynch mobs without the benefit of a trial. In 1929, however, the number fell to seven (al-

(Left) Mafia leader Al Capone in 1928. Gangsters gained influence during Prohibition, when it was illegal to buy or sell alcohol. Criminals, called bootleggers, made huge profits in liquor sales.

(Below) Henry Ford behind the wheel of his 1927 Model A. Ford Motor Company, General Motors, and the Chrysler Corporation were all bringing out new, more affordable models of automobiles, whose sales took off during the boom years of the twenties.

though many lynchings may not have been recorded). On the other hand, during the 1920s, an African-American literary movement, the "Harlem Renaissance," or rebirth, attracted public notice. Through books and poems, writers such as Langston Hughes, Claude McKay, and James Weldon Johnson revealed their bitterness at the way black people were treated in racially segregated America. They also told of their pride in their heritage.

Despite these problems, most Americans thought their future looked bright. They were eager to enjoy the good life, to receive all the benefits the American economy could give them. In 1929 Americans bought 23 percent more clothing, food, and gadgets than they had six years earlier and 33 percent more cars, appliances, and furniture. The recently developed installment plan made it easy for them to shop even when they did not have enough money to pay for their purchases. All they had to do was agree to put down some part of the purchase price at once and pay off the rest in monthly installments. Advertisers now told people that to keep up with their neighbors they had to own the latest model car, radio, washing machine, and refrigerator, even if the old ones still worked. Thanks to inventor Clarence Birdseye, mothers could now prepare quick meals using frozen foods in their shiny up-to-date kitchens. They could even buy milk in waxed cartons instead of glass bottles. Garbage disposals were also sold for the first time. Despite all the conveniences of modern life, however, the nation's homemakers would have to manage without air conditioning. In 1929, it was installed in a Texas office building, but households had to await the future.

Automobiles had become so popular that production expanded from 1.5 million vehicles in 1921 to 4.7 million in 1929. In the 1928 presidential campaign, Herbert Hoover's supporters had even boasted that there would soon be "a car in every backyard." To boost sales, Henry Ford had introduced the dashing Model A automobile in 1927 to replace his practical and durable Model T. Not to be outdone by Ford, Walter P. Chrysler, *Time* magazine's Man of the Year, brought out the first Plymouth and De Soto cars in 1929. If Americans tired of travel by car, they could travel by commercial propeller-driven airplanes, with routes covering 50,000 miles within the nation. There were no coast-to-coast passenger flights yet, but a traveler could get from New York to Los Angeles in forty-six to forty-eight hours by taking the railroad and planes.

Some authors criticized the way Americans lived. They ridiculed people who spent so much time enjoying themselves in foolish ways and measured their success by the number of things they owned. Among others, Sinclair Lewis, F. Scott Fitzgerald, and H. L. Mencken exposed the emptiness of American life in their writings. Their criticisms did not prevent Americans from continuing on their spending sprees.

CHAPTER THREE

"A CRASH IS COMING"

In 1929, about two million Americans owned stocks. They could even keep track of the stock market while traveling to and from Europe because brokers opened branch offices on trans-Atlantic ships. When women felt uncomfortable trading shares in masculine surroundings filled with cigar smoke, they could make their purchases in comfortable hotel rooms set aside for them. Since the beginning of the decade, more and more women had been investing in the stock market. For example, in 1929, women shareholders owned about 55 percent of American Telegraph and Telephone stock. By then, twenty-two Wall Street brokerage firms had women partners, although none yet traded on the floor of the New York Stock Exchange.

Most Americans ignored warnings that the market might collapse. They paid little attention on September 5, 1929, when financial advisor Roger W. Babson warned: "Sooner or later, a crash

In the twenties, women had a stronger presence in business, politics, and society than ever before. They were seen more often in the workplace, played the market, voted, and dressed in a new, freer style.

is coming and it may be terrific." Despite all the publicity Babson received, they were not scared off when the market did indeed drop after his speech. The next day prices continued their upward climb. The effect of his speech on stock prices had shown how unpredictable the market was, but no one seemed to care. The problems that could cause stocks to plunge were overlooked or dismissed as Americans continued on their stock-buying sprees.

Much of the money being poured into Wall Street went into speculation. This was a serious problem. Speculators bought stock only to make profits from changes in the price of the shares. The money they spent on stocks was not a long-term investment that would help businesses develop and expand or create new products and jobs. As a result, speculation did not help the economy grow. The government was afraid to take strong measures to discourage speculation because such actions might make stock prices fall.

By 1929, ordinary people became speculators. They read newspaper stories about nurses, cattlemen, taxi drivers, or hair-dressers who had made fortunes in the stock market. Reporters sometimes made up or exaggerated these success stories. Nevertheless, many inexperienced investors withdrew their life savings and bought stock. To find out which shares to buy or sell, people often relied on tips from their friends who claimed to know stock-brokers. Others consulted astrologers like Evangeline Adams, who made market predictions based on the positions of the planets and the stars. About 100,000 people paid fifty cents a piece for her monthly newsletter forecasting which stocks would rise and fall.

Another problem was created by the low margin, or down payment, required to buy stocks. This fed widespread speculation. In 1929, buyers had to pay only 10 percent of the purchase price of their shares and took loans from the broker for the rest, using their partially paid-for stocks as security for the loans. For $500, a person could buy $5000 worth of stocks. This made it possible for the average wage earner as well as the rich executive to become shareholders. When stock prices were rising, the loans could easily be repaid out of profits from the sale of the shares. The government was reluctant to raise the margin requirement, fearing this would discourage sales and panic the market.

Once the price of the stocks started to spiral downward, however, brokers demanded that the loans be repaid immediately or the shares would be sold before they became worthless. Like many small shareholders, Wall Street shoeshine man Pat Bologna had bought $5000 worth of stock on margin by October 1929. Since he could not afford to pay off his loan to keep his shares, he asked his broker to sell them. All he got back was $1700. Others were not as lucky. They tried to meet their brokers' demands so they could hold on to their stocks. They borrowed money from relatives or rushed to sell their watches and jewelry. Usually, they raised too little cash, too late. The rapid sale of stocks held on margin fed the market downturn and contributed to the severity of the Crash.

Unethical practices of bankers, businessmen, and Wall Street traders also contributed to the stock market's increasing instability. A group of investors might form a pool, and manipulate the price of stocks for profit. In 1928, Michael Meehan, an expert on Radio Corporation of America (RCA) stock, invited some of his wealthy friends to contribute to a pool to buy shares of RCA. They collected $12.6 million and gradually bought large blocks of the stock. It climbed from $81.75 per share on March 12 to $109.25 on March 16. During those four days, newspaper reporters and radio broadcasters reported the stock's rising price. This encouraged the public to buy shares, causing prices to go even higher. On March 17, the pool's managers quietly began to sell off their shares and by the time all of them were sold on March 21, the stock had dropped back to $92.50. The pool's profit was $4.9 million. Others found that they had bought overpriced shares whose value then dropped suddenly.

Many shady dealings were conducted by holding companies, organizations that bought shares in specific industries in order to control them. The most notorious was Samuel Insull's public utility empire in the Midwest. It eventually controlled sixty-five gas and electric companies that made and sold power in thirty-two states. Insull's complicated financial arrangements made it difficult to trace who owned the power companies or to figure out who was responsible for their operations. For example, Insull Utility Investments held a majority of shares in Middle West Utilities. Middle West, in turn, controlled the National Electric Power Company, which owned the most stock in Seaboard Service Company, which was the major shareholder of the Tidewater Power Company of North Carolina.

Insull used a number of questionable methods to make money. For example, in 1929, he had sold four times more stock than his company was worth by printing extra shares and finding buyers for them. This was known as "watering stock," from a trick cattlemen used. To get more money for their livestock, they let the cows drink their fill before being weighed for sale. Insull even owned the company that printed the stock certificates, the Lincoln Printing Company. As a result of his schemes, Insull Utility Investments increased in value from $1 million to $4 million in just a few months.

Insull also manipulated stock by having his holding companies buy shares in one another for more than the stocks were worth so that each could claim a profit. By mid-1929, Insull created Corporation Securities Company of Chicago as a co-equal superholding company. Insull Utility Investments and this new company then bought shares of each other. This has been described as the "parrot-birdcage" method, using a husband who owned a birdcage and a wife who had a parrot as examples. The husband sells the cage to her for $150 more than he paid for it. She sells him the parrot for $150 more than it cost her. Together the family then claims to make a profit of $300!

State governments regulated utilities by setting the amount of profits they could earn based on the value of what the company owned. Through the "parrot-birdcage" method, many of Insull's companies made it seem as if they owned many shares of valuable stock so that state regulators would let them make greater profits. Though weakened by the Crash, Insull's empire did not collapse until late 1931, when heavy trading brought down the price of the overvalued shares. In 1932, Insull was charged with fraud but acquitted after a lengthy trial.

*W*HILE THE STOCK MARKET continued to rise, no one seemed to care that the nation's economy was in trouble. There were a number of weaknesses. For one thing, wealth was very unevenly distributed in the United States. In 1929, 5 percent of all Americans were rich, owning half of all the wealth in the nation and earning four times more than most workers. Between 1919 and 1929, workers had increased the number of goods they made by about 43 percent, but wages did not increase. Who would be able to buy all of the items being made? Wealthy Americans bought nearly one third of all the goods and services sold, but this was not enough.

Two out of every five workers earned less than $1,500 a year, so they had little to spend. Unions were weak and could do little to get pay raises for their members or prevent layoffs. For example, in 1926, they were unable to save northern coal miners' jobs when coal companies shifted their operations to the South. To better compete with oil and gas producers, the mine owners cut costs by moving to a region where they could hire cheap, nonunion workers.

Farmers were in trouble throughout the 1920s. Crop prices fell as farmers from other nations began to compete with Americans in world markets. This hurt U.S. cotton and wheat growers who relied on overseas sales. Also, American eating habits had changed. People no longer bought as much beef, flour, and pork. Faced with falling prices and changing needs, farmers tried to sell more crops.

They borrowed money to buy tractors and other costly equipment to increase their harvests. They only succeeded in driving prices lower. In 1928–1929, South Dakota corn sold for three cents a bushel, less than it cost to grow it. Soon farmers could not make their loan payments.

Without large increases in wages or major price reductions, Americans could not afford to buy all the goods being made. Businesses depended on foreign markets to dispose of their goods. Overseas sales were disappointing, however, because many nations were dealing with their own economic problems and lacked the money to buy American products.

During the summer of 1929, automobile manufacturing and housing construction, so crucial to American prosperity for the past ten years, slowed down. Department store sales also declined. These were warning signs of trouble ahead.

Women make canvas gloves in a textile mill. Only a small portion of Americans experienced the prosperity and freedom of the twenties. Many Americans did repetitive jobs in factories and mills, where hours were long and wages were very low.

With a stock market built on such shaky foundations as speculation, low margin rates, and unsound trading practices, all it took was the sale of a large block of shares for prices to start falling. Then a panicky public tried to cash in its stocks, and on October 29, 1929, the market crashed. Reeling from the crash, the already weakened American economy soon collapsed, leaving many Americans to face an uncertain future.

CHAPTER FOUR

"BROTHER, CAN YOU SPARE A DIME?"

On October 30, 1929, ninety-year-old John D. Rockefeller, Sr., the wealthy oil tycoon, tried to reassure the public by announcing, "My son and I have for some days been purchasing sound common stocks." Comedian Eddie Cantor reacted by saying, "Who else has any money left?" Some Americans did, including businessmen Norton Simon and Joseph Kennedy, father of President John F. Kennedy. They had sold off their stock before the Crash and would buy back shares at bargain prices in the 1930s. Most people, however, were not as fortunate.

The Crash jolted average Americans awake. No longer would they dream of getting rich quickly by speculating in stocks. Now they wondered whether they would earn enough money to buy food, pay the rent, or purchase clothes for their growing children. What would they do if they lost their jobs? Without savings, what would happen when they were too old to work? What if they became sick? There wasn't any "safety net" of government programs to give money to the jobless, welfare payments to needy families, health insurance to the elderly and the poor, or social security to retired or disabled people.

To make ends meet, many people tried to withdraw the money they had put aside in savings accounts, but thousands of banks failed after the Crash. Bankers had lost so much money on risky loans that they could not pay their depositors. One dramatic example was the New York branch of the Bank of the United States which closed in December 1930, wiping out the savings of nearly half a million people. No one had yet thought up a system of government insurance to protect bank accounts.

Depositors create a "run" on the New York branch of the Bank of the United States. When the branch closed in 1930, half a million people lost their savings.

Between 1929 and 1932, the United States economy stopped growing. Americans found themselves in the midst of the Great Depression as the economy came to a stop. With unsold goods on the shelves, stores placed fewer orders from manufacturers. Everyone who had the money to buy a car or a radio already owned one. Despite a drop in prices, Henry Ford could not sell many cars and had to shut down his newest factory. The government gave Americans a tax cut to encourage them to buy products, but it did not make much difference. Wage earners who made $4,000 a year had their taxes reduced from $5.63 to $1.88, which brought them only $3.75 in extra spending money. Since people made fewer purchases, production fell by 28 percent in 1930 and by more than 50 percent in 1932. By 1932 the amount of money paid to workers was 60 percent less than it had been in 1929.

People were reluctant to spend the money they had left. Instead of buying the latest-model appliances, Americans made do or did without. Sometimes they swapped with others for what they needed. Women would patch up clothing for their families and pass it on from child to child. The soles of worn-out shoes were replaced with pieces of rubber cut from used tires. Women would stare longingly at store windows that featured the latest styles. They noticed that dress hemlines had fallen along with stock prices. Longer hair, tiny waistlines, and ruffles became fashionable, too. Even women who could afford new clothing dressed somberly.

When families could no longer keep up installments on the furniture they had purchased, the store took it back, even if there were only one or two payments left to make. People who could not pay their rent or keep up payments on their homes found themselves out on the street. Thousands of families lost their homes, while other houses and apartments stood dark and empty. Sometimes their neighbors would offer them shelter and store some of their possessions. Otherwise, they joined the other homeless who slept under bridges or camped out in public parks.

Shanty towns sprang up in big cities and small towns all across the nation. People built shacks out of cardboard boxes, pieces of wood, and anything else they could find. To express their disgust with the president, they called these makeshift settlements Hoovervilles. Single men often sneaked onto freight trains and traveled the country in a fruitless search for a better life. At the towns along the rail lines, they did odd jobs in exchange for food or cast-off clothing.

"No one has starved," President Hoover announced, but in 1931, there were twenty known cases of starvation in New York City. Soup kitchens and bread lines were a common sight in cities and towns throughout the nation. Children were often sent out to get free food for their families after school. Years later, one of those children remembered that in her Oklahoma town, the man ladling the soup would "dip the greasy, watery stuff off of the top. So we'd ask him to please dip down to get some meat and potatoes from the bottom of the kettle. But he wouldn't do it."

During the early 1930s, Americans still found ways to escape from their difficulties—at least for a few hours. In 1931 the Empire State Building opened to visitors. For a nickel or a dime, people could go to the movies. In 1932, Charles U. Yeager introduced "Bank Night" at Colorado movie theaters, holding a lottery for money and prizes to attract audiences. The idea quickly spread to other states. Americans also entered contests in the hope of winning needed cash or prizes. Two million people tried to solve puzzles sponsored by Old Gold cigarettes to win $100,000. Dance

Many people who lost their homes were forced to build temporary shelters from scrap wood and cardboard. Shanty-towns, called Hoovervilles in mockery of the president, sprang up across the country— near oil wells in Oklahoma City (left) and along the East River in New York City (below).

(Right) Lighthearted competitions of the twenties gave way to desperate contests for prize money during the Depression. These couples are competing in a dance marathon to determine who can remain on their feet the longest.

marathons became the latest craze, offering prize money to couples willing to spend thousands of hours moving sleepily about the floor to outlast their competitors.

Many Americans, however, became less social. Millions of telephones were disconnected when bills were overdue. Church attendance dropped because people could not contribute to the collection plate or lacked the busfare to get to services. Going out was embarrassing to families with shabby clothing. Even inviting guests for visits was difficult because people were unable to afford refreshments.

So people found things to do at home, alone. They tuned in to the comedy routines of Jack Benny or George Burns and Gracie Allen on the radio. Soap operas were created to distract radio listeners from their own worries. Fans of comic strips were treated to the arrival of Blondie in 1930 and detective Dick Tracy in 1931.

FARMERS AND WORKERS were especially hard hit by the Great Depression. The price of farm crops dropped even farther after the Crash. Then a severe dry spell caused the topsoil in midwestern states to blow away, creating the Dust Bowl, and leaving many farmers without crops to sell. Rural banks could no longer afford to be lenient to farmers who did not keep up their loan payments. Their farms were sold at auction. It was tragic for the farmers. "A doll, a couple of books, a basket with the Bible in it, the kids' wagon. . . . Here you had the whole history of the family in all this junk. People pawing over it and buying it for a penny on the dollar." Many farm families in Dust Bowl states such as Oklahoma packed their few remaining possessions into cars and drove west, to California, hoping to find work.

*A family camps out on the road, having lost everything in
the Dust Bowl. A severe drought in the Midwest conspired
with the collapse of the economy to spell disaster for farmers.*

By the end of 1930, some 6 million Americans were out of work. By 1932, that number had doubled. Blacks were the first to be laid off. In many cases, black women supported their families by working as housemaids. Unions were still too weak to help members keep their jobs. To prevent more men from losing their paychecks, workers at Republic Steel, Standard Oil, and the Baltimore and Ohio Railroad shared their jobs so that each could work a day or two a week. This did not, however, reduce company costs or give workers enough money to make more purchases. In 1931, in the hope of putting men back to work, a number of cities passed laws against hiring married women as city workers. The federal government briefly refused to give wages to both husbands and wives on its payroll.

E. Y. "Yip" Harburg wrote the words to a song called "Brother, Can You Spare a Dime?" that expressed the public's mood. He explained that the song's title was taken from a popular phrase used in the early thirties by people asking passersby for a handout.

Harburg went on to say that the song wasn't only about handouts; it was also about human dignity. "This is the man who says: 'I built the railroads. I built that tower. I fought your wars. I was the kid with the drum. Why in hell should I be standing in line now? What happened to all this wealth I created?' " These were questions everyone was asking. Most people wanted to work, but there was little work to be had. People were embarrassed to receive charity. They wanted to earn money and tended to blame themselves rather than the Depression for their inability to find work. As the years passed, the jobless began to blame the government instead.

An unemployed man sells an apple to a congressman
in front of the Capitol Building in 1930.

Private and local government groups were able to offer work to some Americans. In the fall of 1930, the International Apple Shippers Association had so much unsold fruit that it offered to let jobless Americans buy crates of apples on credit to sell on street corners at 5 cents each. By the end of November, there were more than 6,000 apple peddlers in New York City. They became a lasting symbol of the Great Depression. In 1931 a New York group put 32,000 people to work planting trees and maintaining buildings.

Some of the jobless took in piecework. For example, women worked at home sewing clothing. They were paid for each item, or piece, they completed. Others took jobs as door-to-door salespeople whose earnings depended on the number of sales they made. Outfits like the Fuller Brush Company found that their profits rose because of the desperate and talented people who sold their products.

Some thirty million Americans depended on private charities and state and local government relief efforts. Only New York State had a Department of Welfare. Cities could not collect taxes and had to cut the wages of the police, teachers, and firefighters. By the fall of 1931, Chicago had about 600,000 people out of work and ran out of money for relief. In Detroit, Michigan people received 15 cents a day until the city used up its welfare funds. Relief programs and private charities could no longer handle the problem. Something had to be done.

CHAPTER FIVE

"WE HAVE NOW PASSED THE WORST"

After the Crash, President Herbert Hoover repeatedly insisted that things would soon get better. In March 1930, he announced: "We have now passed the worst and with continued unity of effort shall rapidly recover." Privately, he may have had doubts, but his public statements were very encouraging. He even asked comedian Will Rogers to make jokes to cheer the people and urged entertainer Rudy Vallee to sing happy songs. Neither one responded, and things did not get better.

Americans asked the president to help them, but the federal government had never created jobs to help people, housed the homeless, or fed the starving. Hoover wasn't willing to start such novel programs. He sincerely believed that the nation's lawmakers and officials should not interfere in the lives of its citizens. Hoover felt that such interference would cause people to lose their freedom and their ability to help themselves, two qualities that had made the nation great. He wanted the government to serve as an umpire to make sure that people had equality of opportunity and acted for the common good. He thought that if everyone cooperated, the economy would automatically adjust and correct itself. If businesses started producing more, the Depression would soon disappear. That is what had happened when the economy had slowed down in the past. His principles were widely accepted before the Crash but soon proved to be inadequate.

The president also turned down federal employment and relief programs because they would require more government spending. He wanted to keep the government budget balanced. Like many other Americans of his day, Hoover felt that government should not go into debt. It should not spend more money than it took in. Most economists, however, believe that his efforts to balance the budget only made the Depression worse.

Hoover took actions consistent with his beliefs. At his suggestion, Congress passed a law reducing taxes so Americans would have more money to spend. To keep the Depression from spreading, he called meetings of business executives and urged them keep up production, prices, and wages. He asked the government to make it easy for them to borrow money. He thought these recommendations would help businesses get back on track and prevent more workers from losing their jobs.

To help farmers in the Dust Bowl, Hoover created the National Drought Relief Committee in 1930 to provide them with information. Funds to help them keep their farms, however, had to be raised locally by volunteers. The local committees did not have enough money to distribute to debt-ridden farmers, though. When banks could not afford to extend their loans, they seized farms as payment. Nevertheless, Hoover stuck to his belief that emergencies such as this should be handled by "mutual self-help through voluntary giving." In 1931, he finally made more funds available to local banks through Federal Farm Loans to help farmers stay on their land. However, he rejected suggestions to limit the acreage farmers planted in an effort to raise prices. He felt the government had no right to tell farmers what to do.

In 1930, Hoover had welcomed passage of the Smoot-Hawley Tariff Act. It protected American businesses from foreign competition by raising fees the government collected on goods made abroad and sold in the United States. However, this law made foreign products more expensive. As a result, other nations had difficulty selling their goods to Americans. They could not make the money they needed to buy American products or pay their debts to American banks.

The Crash had weakened many European economies, and the Smoot-Hawley tariff made their problems worse. Although Hoover blamed the European nations for the failure of the American economy to recover, in 1931, he decided to help them. He declared that foreign governments who owed money to the United States would not have to make any loan payments for a year. "This is perhaps the most daring statement I ever thought of issuing," the president told his private secretary.

While this generous move was hailed in Europe, it came too late to be effective. What's more, it hurt American banks. As a result of World War I, they had loaned millions of dollars abroad and unless they got their money back, many now faced the possibility of closing. Hoover responded by holding more meetings with bankers and business and insurance executives. He told them that "senseless bankers' panic and public fear" was all that was holding the country back from recovery. He urged them to make more loans to get the economy started up again through a National Credit Corporation.

By 1932, Hoover took further steps to rescue the banks and corporations in the hope that these measures would also help the farmers and workers. At his urging, Congress provided funds to banks and insurance companies so they could stay in business without having to call in the rest of the loans they had made. In February 1932, the lawmakers created the Reconstruction Finance Corporation (RFC) to lend more money to banks and insurance companies, and to railroads. These programs did not violate the president's principles.

Although conditions had worsened, the president clung to his beliefs. "The humanism of our system demands the protection of the suffering and the unfortunate. It places that prime responsibility upon the individual for the welfare of his neighbor." Hoover still refused to let the government give relief directly to the unemployed. He claimed that federal handouts would destroy the people's desire to help themselves. Many Americans sincerely felt that welfare programs were bad for the poor, believing that the needy would be unwilling to look for jobs or to accept work at low wages if they were given money. The president continued to urge local governments and private charities to provide for the poor. This is why a 1930 committee on unemployment, reorganized into the President's Organization for Unemployment Relief (POUR) in 1931, simply encouraged Americans to help one another.

In June 1932, Hoover asked Congress for a modest tax increase because the government's expenses were greater than the money it was taking in. He thought that income taxes for the rich and taxes on inheritances might be raised. What he got instead was "the largest peacetime tax increase in history." Congress had refused to cut the government's expenses as Hoover had wanted. Now, in addition to income taxes, taxes were collected on chewing gum, soft drinks, and gasoline as well as such luxury items as yachts and jewelry. These measures hurt the poor as well as the rich.

To keep the government from going into further debt, the president would only support public works programs that would pay for themselves, such as the building of bridges and roads. By charging tolls, the costs of such construction could be recovered. Many states, however, had already exhausted their legal limit to borrow money for such public works. Finally, in July 1932, Hoover signed a law allowing the RFC to make loans to local governments for more public works. More importantly, the law provided up to $300 million to support local relief efforts, but the federal government still did not aid people directly. By May 1933, about $280 million had been loaned to forty-two states, but it was far too little. When the governor of Pennsylvania asked for a $45 million loan, he received $11 million, which gave each jobless person in his state an added 3 cents a day.

*D*URING THE SPRING OF 1932, some 15,000 unemployed veterans of World War I marched to Washington, D.C., from all over the country. They were determined to stay in the nation's capital until Congress voted them their bonus. In 1924 a grateful Congress had given each World War I veteran a bonus certificate, amounting to about $1,000, to be cashed in twenty years later. The out-of-work veterans wanted their money now. The District's chief of police, Pelham G. Glassford, felt sorry for the former servicemen. He collected money for them, secured tents for them to sleep in,

Unemployed World War I veterans sleep on the grounds of the Capitol. This "Bonus Army" came to demand early payment on the thousand-dollar bonus promised to each of them by Congress.

Children solicit money at one of the bonus camps in Washington, D.C.

and found places for them to wash up. He visited the men, joking with them and talking about their wartime adventures. There were twenty-three camps in the district's parks and abandoned buildings. At first, the camps were a tourist attraction, and visitors brought the ex-soldiers food and cigarettes. Hoover and his advisers, however, feared the veterans would riot. Glassford was told to remove them but failed to take action. His police force was vastly outnumbered by the "Bonus Army."

When the Senate voted down a bonus bill, half the veterans went home. The rest stayed on because they had no place to go or no money to leave town. Then Congress passed a law to let them borrow against their bonuses to pay for transportation home. Some former servicemen remained, still hoping to see the president and plead their cause. They camped out on Anacostia Flats and occupied vacant government buildings. In late July, they were ordered to leave government buildings, and a fight erupted, possibly stirred up by agitators. Two men were killed and several policemen were injured. Secretary of War Patrick Hurley had been looking for just such an incident as an excuse to oust the veterans. At his request, Hoover called out the army. The troops, led by General Douglas MacArthur, went to Anacostia Flats, where they forced the veterans to leave and burned their shacks. President Hoover commented, "Thank God, we still have a government that knows how to deal with a mob."

Americans felt it was time for a change. In the election of 1932, they gave Democratic candidate Franklin Delano Roosevelt an overwhelming victory over Republican President Hoover. Roosevelt won in forty-two of the forty-eight states, receiving over seven million more votes than Hoover.

On the campaign trail in 1932, Franklin Delano Roosevelt shakes hands with a miner. Roosevelt believed more strongly than Hoover did that the government should take a much more active role in lifting the nation out of the Depression.

CHAPTER SIX

"THE ONLY THING WE HAVE TO FEAR IS FEAR ITSELF"

On Black Monday, October 19, 1987, the value of stocks fell by 22.6 percent, the greatest one-day decline since 1914. The next day, however, share prices recovered and started to climb once again. In 1990, more than 470 savings and loans banks failed and 500 more were in trouble. The federal government promptly came to their aid, and depositors got their money back. In both instances, Americans were spared another Great Depression. What made the difference? The economy in 1987 and 1990 was healthier than it had been in 1929, the federal government was willing to act quickly to avoid a disaster, and the safeguards passed in the 1930s had worked.

In 1933, under the leadership of President Roosevelt, Congress took steps to prevent another major stock market crash and its disastrous effects. Lawmakers passed Roosevelt's New Deal, a program of laws to reform the economy, promote recovery, and

The WPA gave jobs to writers, photographers, sculptors, and painters. The government hired William Gropper to paint this mural of WPA workers building a dam.

give relief to the needy. Among the reforms was Federal Deposit Insurance, which guaranteed that people could collect the money they placed in savings and checking accounts if banks failed.

As a result of a 1932 investigation into the nation's stock markets, Congress set up the Securities and Exchange Commission in 1934 to regulate them, supervise the sale of new stock, and protect the public from fraud. Such practices as watering stock became illegal. To discourage wild speculation, the government also raised margin rates to 50 percent or more, depending on economic conditions. In 1935, a new law placed many restrictions on public utility

holding companies and, after 1938, limited them to business operations directly related to selling power.

A number of laws were passed to promote recovery. For example, in 1933, the Tennessee Valley Authority provided government funds for flood control and low-cost electricity to benefit people in seven states. Under the 1933 Agriculture Adjustment Act and the 1936 Soil Conservation Act, the government paid farmers to cut production and take better care of their lands. From 1933 to 1935, businesses and industries were encouraged to draw up codes of fair competition for government approval. These codes permitted

[53]

them to temporarily limit production and fix prices, practices previously outlawed. In 1935 Congress passed the National Labor Relations Act recognizing the right of workers to form unions to represent them in their dealings with employers. In 1938, the Fair Labor Standards Act limited the maximum number of hours people could work and set minimum wages. Despite these and other measures, economic recovery did not take place until World War II.

The New Deal committed the federal government to give relief to needy Americans. A number of programs were created to put Americans back to work. For example, the Works Progress Administration, set up in 1935, hired artists, writers, and actors as well as construction workers and engineers to work on government-funded projects. Some painted murals, collected oral histories, or put on plays for the public while others built roads, bridges, or airports. For the first time in the nation's history, the government accepted direct responsibility for the well-being of its citizens. In 1935, Congress passed the Social Security Act, providing benefits for the retired, elderly, disabled, needy with dependent children, and jobless. The lawmakers had created a "safety net" to protect Americans.

As a result of the Great Depression and the New Deal, American attitudes changed. Now, citizens expected the government to keep the economy running smoothly and to help them in times of distress. In the decades to come, this required more and more government spending. Yet those who had lived through the Great Depression were still insecure. They never regained their self-confidence. No matter how successful they became, they remembered the hard times and worried about the future. They feared that another economic collapse might take away everything they had.

So far, government safeguards have prevented another Great Depression, but as Black Monday of 1987 showed, they cannot keep the stock market from crashing. They can only cushion its effects. Stock market prices reflect people's hopes and fears. While hope may encourage the market to soar to new heights as people buy more and more stock, fear may cause it to tumble in a downward spiral as people panic and sell off all the stock they own. In 1933, when he took the oath of office, Franklin Roosevelt said, "The only thing we have to fear is fear itself." His message is still timely. Any major news story—such as American troops going to war in the Persian Gulf or an unexpected rise in the price of food and clothing—may set off a surge of buying or selling of stocks. Those are the risks of investing, and people who put money in the stock market must be prepared to accept them.

Chronology

1928   Herbert C. Hoover is elected president of the United States.

1929   The stock market crashes on Black Tuesday (October 29).

1930   Hoover signs the Smoot-Hawley Tariff Act, which sets the highest rates on imported goods in the nation's history.

1932   The creation of the Reconstruction Finance Corporation. The forced removal of the Bonus Veterans from Washington, D.C. Franklin D. Roosevelt is elected president of the United States.

1933   Start of Roosevelt's New Deal, a program of laws to bring economic recovery and reform.

1934   Creation of the Federal Securities and Exchange Commission.

1935   Roosevelt signs the Social Security Act into law.

1936   Roosevelt is re-elected to the presidency. He is elected for a third term in 1940.

1941   The United States enters World War II.

Glossary

Bid: An offer to buy a stock, usually at the current market price or lower.

Bonds: Notes promising to repay with interest money lent to businesses or government.

Brokers (also stockbrokers): People who arrange stock and bond trades for the public.

Holding company: A company that owns enough stock in another company to control it. Holding companies do not make or sell products.

Interest: The amount of money lenders charge borrowers.

Investors: People who buy stocks or bonds in the hope that their value will increase.

Margin: Buying stocks on credit, where buyers pay only part of the price of the stock and a broker lends them the rest. If the price of the stock goes up, buyers can pay the broker back from profits made after the stock is sold. If the price of the stock goes down, brokers often sell the stock at a loss to the buyer.

Pools: Groups of speculators who manipulate the price of stocks by heavily investing in one industry to encourage others to buy its shares. Once the price goes up enough, they sell off their shares for a large profit.

Public utilities: Gas and electric companies, usually regulated by the states, that make and sell power.

Share: One of the equal portions into which the stock of a company is divided.

Speculator: A person who buys or sells shares in the hope of making a profit from changes in stock prices.

Stock: A share in the ownership of a company.

Stock market: A place where shares in companies are bought and sold.

Bibliography

*Books of interest to young readers

Allen, Frederick Lewis. *Only Yesterday*. New York: Bantam Books, 1959.
————. *The Big Change*. New York: Bantam Books, 1961.
*Anglo, Michael. *Nostalgia Spotlight on the Twenties*. London: Universal Books, Ltd., 1985.
Arnold, Thurman. "The Crash and What It Meant," in *The Aspirin Age 1919–1940*, ed. by Isabel Leighton. New York: Simon & Schuster, 1949, pp. 214–231.
Bird, Caroline. *The Invisible Scar*. New York: David McKay, 1966.
Butterfield, Roger. *The American Past*. New York: Simon & Schuster, 1947.
*Clinton, Susan. *Herbert Hoover*. Chicago: Childrens Press, 1988.
Galbraith, John Kenneth. *The Great Crash 1929*. Boston: Houghton Mifflin Riverside Press, 1961.
Garraty, John A. *The Great Depression*. San Diego: Harcourt Brace Jovanovich, 1986.
*Glassman, Bruce. *The Crash of Twenty-Nine and the New Deal*. Morristown, N.J.: Silver Burdett, 1985.

*Meltzer, Milton. *Brother, Can You Spare a Dime: The Great Depression 1929– 1933.* New York: Facts on File, 1990.

*Polikof, Barbara G. *Herbert Hoover, Thirty-First President of the United States.* Ada, Okla.: Garrett Educational Corp., 1990.

Schlesinger, Arthur M., Jr. "The First Hundred Days of the New Deal," in *The Aspirin Age 1919–1940,* ed. by Isabel Leighton. New York: Simon & Schuster, 1949, pp. 275–296.

*Schraff, Anne E. *The Great Depression and the New Deal: America's Economic Collapse and Recovery.* New York: Franklin Watts, 1990.

Sloat, Warren. *1929: America Before the Crash.* New York: Macmillan, 1979.

Smith, Gene. *The Shattered Dream: Herbert Hoover and the Great Depression.* New York: William Morrow, 1970.

*Stein, Richard. *The Great Depression.* Chicago: Childrens Press, 1993.

*Tames, Richard. *The 1930s.* New York: Franklin Watts, 1991.

*———. *The 1920s.* New York: Franklin Watts, 1991.

Thomas, Gordon and Max Morgan-Witts. *The Day the Bubble Burst: A Social History of the Wall Street Crash of 1929.* Garden City: Doubleday & Co., 1979.

Turkel, Studs. *Hard Times: An Oral History of the Great Depression.* New York: Pantheon Books, 1970.

Warren, Harris G. *Herbert Hoover and the Great Depression.* New York: Oxford University Press, 1959.

Watkins, T. H. *The Great Depression: America in the 1930s.* Boston: Little, Brown and Co., 1993.

United States Department of Commerce. Bureau of the Census. *Historical Statistics of the United States Colonial Times to 1970.* 2 vols. Washington, D.C.: Government Printing Office, 1975.

Index

About the Author

Barbara Silberdick Feinberg holds a Ph.D. in political science from Yale University. Her more recent books are *Watergate: Scandal in the White House*, *American Political Scandals Past and Present*, *The National Government*, *State Governments*, *Local Governments*, *Words in the News: A Student's Dictionary of American Government and Politics*, *Harry S. Truman*, *John Marshall: The Great Chief Justice*, *Hiroshima and Nagasaki*, *The Cabinet*, and *Electing the President*. She has also written *Marx and Marxism*, *The Constitution: Yesterday, Today, and Tomorrow*, and *Franklin D. Roosevelt, Gallant President*. She is a contributor to *The Young Reader's Companion to American History*.

Mrs. Feinberg lives in New York City with her sons Jeremy and Douglas and two Yorkshire terriers, Katie and Holly. Among her hobbies are growing African violets, collecting antique autographs of historical personalities, and listening to the popular music of the 1920s and 1930s.